African Americans Who Were First

African Americans Who Were First

Joan Potter and Constance Claytor

Illustrated with photographs

Cobblehill Books
Dutton   New York

ABQ- 8080

Library of Congress Cataloging-in-Publication Data
Potter, Joan.
African Americans who were first / Joan Potter and
Constance Claytor.
p.   cm.   Includes index.
Summary: Provides brief biographical sketches of African Americans who
were the first of their race to accomplish a goal in a variety of fields, from
medicine and politics to sports and entertainment.
ISBN 0-525-65246-9
1. Afro-Americans—Biography—Juvenile literature.   [1. Afro-
Americans—Biography.]   I. Claytor, Constance.   II. Title.
E185.96.P684   1997   920′.009296073—dc21
[B]   97-10164   CIP   AC

Published in the United States by Cobblehill Books,
an affiliate of Dutton Children's Books,
a division of Penguin Books USA Inc.,
375 Hudson Street, New York, New York 10014

Designed by Mina Greenstein
Printed in the United States of America
First Edition   10   9   8   7   6   5   4   3   2   1

In memory of my mother,

SHIRLEY JEAN PROPP

who, by her example, taught me to recognize
the value and dignity of people of all races.

— JOAN POTTER

In memory of my mother,

JULIA MITCHELL

a strong, loving woman who overcame her own
hardships and instilled in her four children the
importance of doing our best and loving one another.

—CONSTANCE CLAYTOR

CONTENTS

For individual names and achievements, see Index

INTRODUCTION

The history of African Americans is not separate from what we call American history. To have a complete picture of the history of our country, we must understand the role played by all the people who helped create it. When we were children, the books we read in our classrooms did not record the deeds and contributions of African Americans. It was as though they had played no part in our country's growth.

In writing this book, we wanted you to discover men and women whom we did not learn about at your age. We wanted to introduce you to people you could take pride in and whom you could respect for the things they have done. We hope you will explore further the lives of these pioneers and the many others who were also great achievers.

The best reward for our efforts would be for you to share what you learn with your family and friends, and to let the lives of these courageous people guide you in setting your own goals.

—Joan Potter and Constance Claytor

THE FIRST
AFRICAN AMERICANS

The first Africans in our country arrived in the English colony at Jamestown, Virginia, aboard a Dutch ship in 1619. These twenty African men and women came here as indentured servants. They had agreed to work for a specific number of years and then were supposed to be set free. Some Africans did gain their freedom, but laws were later passed that turned black servants into slaves for life.

For many years, Africans had been brought as slaves to islands in the Caribbean—islands that were owned by Spain, England, and France. After 1619, increasing numbers of African men, women, and children were also brought to our country to be sold as slaves. Most had lived along a 3,000-mile coastline in West Africa. They came from many cultures, religions, languages, and traditions. These people were torn from their homes in Africa and taken across the ocean in crowded ships, where they did not have enough food or water or places to lie down. Many died before the trip was over.

In this country, a slave's life was one of hard work. Slaves started working as children and continued until they were old. Children were not allowed to go to school or to learn to read and write. Men, women, and children worked in the fields, took care of farm animals, and were servants in their owners' houses. Some learned skills such as carpentry, leather work, weaving, and bricklaying.

After the first Africans arrived in this country, slavery continued to grow. By 1700, it had completely taken hold in the colonies.

Phillis Wheatley

Phillis Wheatley came from Africa on a slave ship and landed in Boston, Massachusetts, in 1761, when she was about eight years old. She was bought by a rich man named John Wheatley who took her to live with his family. Although Phillis could not speak English when she arrived, the Wheatleys taught her to read and write. She was a very bright child, and she especially loved to write poetry. When she was just a teenager, she wrote a poem about the death of a popular minister, which was reprinted many times. Two years later, the Wheatleys tried to publish a book of her poems, but the publisher did not believe that Phillis was the real poet because she was a slave. With one of the Wheatley sons, she sailed to England, where her book of poems was finally published in 1773. It was the first book to be published by an African American.

After she returned to America, Phillis continued to write poetry. She wrote a poem for George Washington when he was made head of the army in 1775, and he invited her to visit him at his headquarters. But soon after that her life became filled with sadness. One by one, the members of the Wheatley family died, and she was left alone. She married a man who treated her badly, and she had two children who died. She and her third baby both died on the same day in December, 1784.

James Derham

Although he was born a slave in 1762, James Derham grew up to be an outstanding doctor. In Philadelphia, where James lived, his master happened to be a doctor. James worked as his master's assistant, learning how to mix medicines and treat patients. His next two owners were also doctors, and the last one, a Scottish doctor in New Orleans, Louisiana, paid James for being his medical assistant. By the time he was about twenty years old, James was able to save enough money to buy his freedom. He opened his own medical office, where he had both African-American and white patients. He was the country's first African-American doctor, and after a few years he was considered one of the best doctors in New Orleans.

On a visit to Philadelphia, James Derham met Dr. Benjamin Rush, one of the country's leading doctors. Rush took an interest in Derham's career and convinced him to move back to Philadelphia. Dr. Derham gained great respect from the other doctors in that city, and became known throughout the country as an expert on the ways that climate affects disease. Despite his success, in 1801 the New Orleans city council told him he could no longer practice in that city because he did not have a medical license. He died within a few years.

Benjamin Banneker

Benjamin Banneker was born on a small tobacco farm near Baltimore, Maryland, in 1731. As a child, he attended a Quaker school near his home, where he was the only African-American student. Benjamin was always interested in mathematics and mechanics. He put this interest to work when he was about twenty-two years old by building the first clock in the American colonies. He figured out how to make it by examining a pocket watch, a picture of a clock, and a geometry book. His clock was carved entirely of wood and struck the hours. It ran for more than forty years.

When Benjamin Banneker was fifty years old, he began to study astronomy—the stars, planets, and other heavenly bodies. He spent many nights outdoors, wrapped in blankets, looking at the skies. He used his knowledge of astronomy and mathematics to publish an almanac in 1792 that contained helpful information about the rising and setting of the sun and the moon, and weather conditions throughout the year. It was the first scientific book published by an African American.

At about that time, Banneker was chosen as a surveyor on a team that laid out the design of the nation's capital in Washington, D.C. He was able to reproduce the original map from memory. He helped pick the site for the Capitol Building and the White House and plan the avenues, circles, and parks. A stone marking one of the boundaries of the District of Columbia was named in his honor.

Alexander Twilight

Alexander Twilight was born in 1795 in Bradford, Vermont, where his father, Ichabod, was a farmer. When he was just a young boy, Alexander was indentured to a nearby farmer, which meant he was forced to work on that farm for a set period of time. When he was twenty years old, he finally managed to leave the farm and entered a school called Randolph Academy. He went on to study at Middlebury College in Vermont, where he earned a Bachelor of Arts degree in 1823, becoming the first African-American college graduate. The leaders of Middlebury College were so proud of him that they later named a building in his honor.

After his graduation, Alexander became a schoolteacher and a preacher in upstate New York. In 1829, he went to Brownington, Vermont, to serve as the minister of the Congregational Church and a school principal. The town's high school, Brownington Academy, was a two-story wooden building with no dormitory. Students who came from far away had to live with families in town. Somehow Alexander Twilight managed to get the money to build a huge stone building where students could live. It had bedrooms, classrooms, a kitchen, and a dining room. It was named Athenian Hall. Some people said that Twilight cut the stone blocks out of nearby fields and put up the building himself with only the help of an ox.

Twilight retired as principal of Brownington Academy in 1855, and

ALEXANDER TWILIGHT

died two years later. His students remembered him as a strict teacher with a colorful personality and a good sense of humor. He and his wife are buried in the village cemetery that overlooks the Academy.

How the Slaves Became Free

During the many years that they were slaves, African Americans responded in different ways. Some felt there was no hope to escape from their masters. Thousands of others risked their lives to run away and gain their freedom. Starting in about 1830, many men and women, both white and black, put their lives in danger by hiding escaped slaves who were traveling to freedom along a network of routes called the Underground Railroad. Friends and supporters offered safe hiding places, food, and clothing to runaway slaves. At the same time, many people spoke out against slavery. They were called Abolitionists because they wanted to abolish slavery.

In April, 1861, the Civil War began. It was a war between the North and the South. The North was opposed to slavery and the South wanted to keep it. The North was called the Union and the South was called the Confederacy. On January 1, 1863, President Abraham Lincoln signed a document called the Emancipation Proclamation that granted freedom to all slaves in the Confederate states. During the war, more than 180,000 African Americans fought with the Union army and at least 37,000 died. The North won the war in 1865, and that same year Congress passed the 13th Amendment to the Constitution, which gave freedom to all African Americans.

The former slaves were given the freedom by law to do things that had once been forbidden. They could now go where they pleased, own their own land, get paid for their work, learn to read and write, and live with their own families. But in spite of their new freedoms, many were not prepared to live on their own. Most lacked the skills needed to get jobs, and it was difficult for them to find food, clothing, and a place to live. However, they were determined to work hard to build their new lives.

William H. Carney

In 1840, when William H. Carney was born in Norfolk, Virginia, his mother was a slave and so was he. Their master died when William was fourteen years old, and they were set free. Two years later, his father moved the family to New Bedford, Massachusetts, where William began studying to become a minister.

In February, 1863, two years after the start of the Civil War, Carney enlisted in the army, joining the Massachusetts 54th Infantry. It was the first black regiment recruited in the North. On July 18 of that year, the soldiers of the regiment led an attack against Fort Wagner, an important Confederate fort in South Carolina. During the battle, the commander of the regiment and many other soldiers were killed.

In the midst of the fighting, Sgt. William Carney was running beside the flag bearer just as the man was shot. Sergeant Carney picked up the flag and led the final attack on the fort. The brave soldier managed to reach the wall protecting the fort, but he was shot twice and badly wounded by Confederate soldiers. As he fell, he held the flag high and passed it to his fellow soldiers, saying, "Boys, it never touched the ground."

William Carney recovered from his wounds and became the first African American to be awarded the Congressional Medal of Honor, the highest military award for bravery.

HARRIET TUBMAN

Harriet Tubman

Harriet Tubman was born about 1820 in Maryland. She was one of eleven children of parents who were slaves. By the time she was five years old, Harriet was working on the plantation as a field hand and a servant. When she was a teenager, her master hit her on the head with a heavy object as she tried to stop him from catching a runaway slave. The injury caused her to suffer for many years.

When Harriet was about twenty-two, she married a man named John Tubman. Four years later, Harriet decided to escape from slavery, but he refused to go with her. So she ran away by herself and traveled up north, where she joined a group of people called Abolitionists, who were working to do away with slavery. Harriet became a "conductor" on the Underground Railroad, helping runaway slaves find safe places to hide.

Harriet made nineteen trips down south and brought back 300 slaves, including her children, her brothers and their families, and her aging parents. Some slaveholders offered a $40,000 reward for her capture, but she was never caught. During the Civil War, Harriet was a spy, a nurse, and a scout. When the war was over, she settled down on a small farm that she had bought in Auburn, New York. She became a strong supporter of women's rights and helped establish a home for poor and elderly African Americans.

After Harriet died of pneumonia in 1913, the residents of Auburn put up a plaque in her honor in the town square. A postage stamp with her picture was issued in February, 1978, the first to feature an African-American woman.

MARY ANN SHADD CARY

Mary Ann Shadd Cary

Mary Ann Shadd Cary was born in 1823 in Wilmington, Delaware. Her parents were not slaves, and they helped other African Americans by offering a hiding place in their home to those who were escaping slavery in the South. Because of her race, Mary Ann was unable to receive an education in Delaware, so she attended a Quaker school in Pennsylvania. After graduation at the age of sixteen, she returned to Wilmington and opened a school for African-American students.

In 1850, the Fugitive Slave Law was passed, which gave slave owners the right to search for and capture runaway slaves. Because they were opposed to the law, Mary Ann and her family moved out of the country to Windsor, Canada. Soon after her arrival there, Mary Ann saw a need for a newspaper for African Americans, especially those who had escaped from slavery. She began publishing a weekly paper called *The Provincial Freeman*. This achievement made her the first African-American newspaperwoman in North America.

Mary Ann Shadd Cary always spoke out against slavery. When President Abraham Lincoln called for men to fight with the Union Army in the Civil War, Mary Ann returned to the United States and helped recruit soldiers for the army. She later moved to Washington, D.C., and enrolled in Howard University Law School. In 1883, she became the second African-American woman in the country to earn a law degree.

Edmonia Lewis

Edmonia Lewis was born about 1843 near Albany, New York. She was the daughter of a Chippewa Indian woman and an African-American man. Edmonia's parents died when she was very young, and her mother's two sisters took her to live with them among the Chippewa Indians. The Chippewas named her Wildfire, and taught her to make baskets and embroidered moccasins. She had a carefree life, swimming, fishing, and playing with the Chippewa children.

Edmonia had a brother who was a gold miner in California. When she was old enough, he arranged for her to enter Oberlin College in Ohio. She studied many things at Oberlin, including drawing and painting. After two years, Edmonia moved to Boston, Massachusetts. She began studying with a local sculptor and soon she was selling her work. She opened her own studio, and created many pieces of sculpture of well-known people.

In 1865, Edmonia sailed to Europe and settled in Rome, Italy, where she continued to sculpt figures of famous people, including Abraham Lincoln, and began work on African-American subjects. As her work became better known, it was praised by people in this country and also other parts of the world. Occasionally, Edmonia returned to the United States to exhibit and sell her works.

Later, her popularity died down and the public began to lose interest in Edmonia Lewis's creations. No one knows just what happened to her or exactly when she died. She seemed to vanish from the art world. Some of her work still survives, though, including her famous

EDMONIA LEWIS

statue called "Forever Free" that shows an African-American man and woman at the moment they heard the news about the freeing of the slaves.

Rebecca Lee Crumpler

Early in her life, Rebecca Lee Crumpler decided that she wanted to "be in a position to relieve the suffering of others." Rebecca was inspired by her aunt, who raised her after she was born in 1833. Rebecca's aunt gave medical care to the people in her community, and Rebecca wanted to follow in her footsteps.

When she was nineteen, she started working as a nurse in Massachusetts. The people she worked for encouraged her to continue her medical education, and at the age of twenty-six she entered New England Medical College in Boston. She was awarded a Doctress of Medicine degree in 1864, and was the first African-American woman in the United States to earn a medical degree.

When the Civil War ended, Dr. Crumpler returned to Richmond, Virginia, the city of her birth. There she provided medical care to the newly freed slaves. After years as a successful doctor in Richmond, she went back to Boston.

In 1883, she published a book on a subject to which she had dedicated her life—health care for women and children. At a time when almost all doctors were men, Rebecca Lee Crumpler was an inspiration for women, and especially African-American women, who wanted to enter the medical profession.

Hiram Rhoades Revels

When he was a young boy in Fayetteville, North Carolina, where he was born in 1822, Hiram Rhoades Revels attended an elementary school run by an African-American woman. He later moved north, where he studied to become a minister. He served as a pastor for churches in several states, and when the Civil War broke out he was living in Baltimore, Maryland. Revels helped in the war effort by organizing two African-American army regiments.

After the war ended, opportunities opened up for African Americans to serve in government offices. Hiram Revels settled in Natchez, Mississippi, where he became active in politics, serving on the city council and in the state senate.

In January, 1870, the Mississippi legislature selected Revels to represent the state in the United States Senate. He was chosen to fill a senate seat that had been empty ever since Jefferson Davis left it in 1861 to become president of the Confederacy. Many white Southerners spoke up and said they didn't want a black man in the Senate. But Revels did not back down, and he became the first African American to serve in the U.S. Senate.

In his first speech before Congress, Revels urged that the state of Georgia not be readmitted to the Union unless it protected the rights of its African-American citizens. He served for a year in the Senate, and later became president of Alcorn University, an African-American college in Mississippi.

MOSES FLEETWOOD WALKER WITH THE TOLEDO MUD HENS

First African American to play
major league baseball

Moses Fleetwood Walker

Moses Fleetwood Walker was born in 1857 in Ohio, where his father was one of the state's first African-American doctors. Fleetwood and his younger brother, Welday, attended Oberlin College. It was the first white college to admit black students. The brothers were the only African-American players on the Oberlin baseball team.

After he graduated, Fleetwood entered the University of Michigan Law School, where he played baseball for two seasons. Then he left school to become a professional ballplayer. The owner of a team called the Toledo Mud Hens had noticed Fleetwood's talent and signed him up as a catcher.

When the Toledo Mud Hens joined the American Association, a major baseball league, in 1884, Moses Fleetwood Walker became the first African-American ballplayer in the majors. But playing on the team was difficult for him, especially when it was traveling in the South. Baseball fans and even his fellow players often shouted insults at him because of his race. After the Toledo team let him go, Fleetwood played for nine more years in the minor leagues.

When he was thirty-seven years old, he left baseball and went to work as a postal clerk in Syracuse, New York. He then returned to Ohio, where he and his brother, Welday, managed an opera house and started a newspaper. He later published a book about African Americans. After he died in 1924, Oberlin College put a headstone on his grave that read: "First Black Major League Baseball Player in U.S.A."

Henry Ossian Flipper

Henry Ossian Flipper, the son of slaves, was born in 1856 in Thomasville, Georgia. His father saved enough money to buy the family's freedom and they moved to the city of Atlanta. Henry studied at Atlanta University until he was chosen to attend the United States Military Academy at West Point, New York.

Other African Americans had entered West Point before Henry, but they were treated so badly by the rest of the cadets that they were forced to leave. Henry Flipper also was mistreated at West Point. The other cadets would not even speak to him during his four years there. But Henry tried to ignore their unkindness. He concentrated on his studies and, in 1877, he became the first African American to graduate from the U.S. Military Academy.

After Flipper graduated, he was assigned to the all-black 10th Cavalry, part of a regiment called the "Buffalo Soldiers," which served throughout the West after the Civil War. In 1882, he was accused of taking money from the army commissary. Although he vowed that he was innocent, he was found guilty and dismissed from the Army.

Henry Flipper went on to have a successful career as a mining engineer. For the rest of his life he tried to clear his name of the charges against him. He died of a heart attack in 1940, still trying to prove his innocence. Finally, in 1978, the army determined that Henry Flipper had not been guilty of any crime and he was given an honorable discharge and a military funeral.

Booker T. Washington

Booker T. Washington was born a slave on a plantation in Virginia about 1856. His mother was a cook on the plantation, but he never knew his father. When he was a child, he worked as a servant in his master's house. After the slaves were freed in 1865, he and his family moved to West Virginia. There he got a job in the home of a rich woman who taught him to read, and he also attended a school for African Americans. He went on to study at Hampton Institute, a college for African Americans in Virginia, where he was an outstanding student. After graduating, he taught school for several years.

In 1881, Washington was chosen to start a new school for African-American students in Tuskegee, Alabama. The first classes were held in an old church and a small building next door. Washington believed that young people should be trained to get jobs. Young men were taught to be farmers, carpenters, painters, plumbers, and blacksmiths, and young women learned cooking, sewing, and nursing. His school grew to be Tuskegee Institute, one of the best African-American colleges in the country.

Washington advised African Americans to try to get ahead by working hard and helping one another. He became a powerful leader in the United States, and after the publication of his autobiography, *Up from Slavery*, his fame spread around the world. He died in 1915, and in 1940, he became the first African American to be honored with his picture on a postage stamp.

BILL PICKETT

Bill Pickett

Bill Pickett, the most famous African-American rodeo cowboy, was born in 1870 outside of Austin, Texas. He attended school until fifth grade when he left to work on ranches near his home. He soon began appearing in rodeos, where he became famous for inventing a special way to wrestle steers to the ground. First, he would jump from his horse onto the steer's back. Then he would grab the steer's horns, twist its head back, sink his teeth into its upper lip, and throw it to the ground. This was called "bulldogging."

By the time he was eighteen years old, Bill Pickett was performing bulldogging and other tricks at shows all around Texas. He went to work on the 101 Ranch in Ponca City, Oklahoma, and in 1907 he joined a famous rodeo called the Miller Brothers 101 Ranch Wild West Show, which toured all around the United States and other countries. Pickett even appeared at Madison Square Garden in New York City.

He performed with the Wild West Show off and on until the late 1920s, and also worked as a rancher. In 1932, on his Oklahoma ranch, he was kicked in the head by a horse that he was trying to tame. The seventy-two-year-old cowboy died eleven days later of a fractured skull. He was buried in Ponca City. In 1971, he became the first African American to be inducted into the Rodeo Cowboy Hall of Fame in Oklahoma City.

DR. DANIEL HALE WILLIAMS

Daniel Hale Williams

The first open-heart operation was performed back in 1893 by an African-American doctor named Daniel Hale Williams. Dr. Williams was born in Pennsylvania in 1856. His father, who was a barber and a minister, died when Daniel was only eleven. The boy went to Wisconsin with his sister and found a job in a barbershop. There he met a doctor who hired him as an assistant and was so impressed by his ability that he helped him get into Chicago Medical School.

Williams earned his medical degree in 1883, and opened an office in Chicago. But because he was an African American, he was not allowed to work in hospitals. He had to operate on his patients in their homes, often on the kitchen or dining room tables.

Dr. Williams was determined to open a hospital where African-American doctors and nurses could be trained and where black patients would receive the best of care. In 1891, his dream came true when he opened Provident Hospital in Chicago, the first African-American-owned hospital in the country.

It was there, two years later, that a man named James Cornish was taken after he was stabbed in the heart. At that time there were no X-rays, antibiotics, or blood transfusions. Yet Dr. Williams opened the patient's chest, repaired the wound, and stitched the incision back together. Mr. Cornish recovered completely, and Dr. Williams became famous throughout the country.

African Americans after Slavery Ended

By the year 1900, many African Americans who had once been slaves were moving out of the South to other parts of the country. They were looking for more opportunities in jobs, housing, and education. African Americans who had been forbidden to read and write when they were slaves were now able to attend school. Many schools and colleges were created especially for African-American students, and black students were allowed to attend some schools that once had been all white.

There were some people, though, who still felt that African Americans should not be treated equally. So some black and white people began to work together to do away with unfair treatment based on a person's race or color. In 1905, an African-American scholar named W.E.B. DuBois started the "Niagara Movement," which was a group of people that met in Niagara Falls and demanded that black Americans be given the same rights as white Americans. This movement grew into the National Association for the Advancement of Colored People (NAACP), which is still active today.

In 1917, the United States entered World War I. About 300,000 African Americans fought in this war before it ended in 1918. But those brave soldiers were not allowed to fight side by side with whites. They served in all-black regiments. The same was true in World War II, where hundreds of thousands of African Americans served in segregated armed forces.

Some African Americans were beginning to be appreciated for their talent in music, art, literature, and the theater. During the 1900s, more and more African-American men and women were recognized for their accomplishments in many fields, from science and medicine to education and government. But the African Americans' struggle for equality would be long and hard. They still had to fight for good jobs and schools and decent places to live.

Bert Williams

This talented singer, dancer, and comedian was born in Antigua, British West Indies, around 1874. His parents named him Egbert Austin Williams, but everyone called him Bert. Even as a child, Bert was a talented musician and singer, and by the time he was twenty he was performing with a troupe of entertainers in San Francisco, California. It was there that he teamed up with a young man named George Walker, and together they traveled across the country to New York City.

In 1903, the two starred on Broadway in a musical called *In Dahomey*. It was the first full-length Broadway show written and performed by African Americans. The show made them famous throughout the world. They starred in two more musicals before George Walker became ill and had to retire.

Bert continued on his own. He became one of the country's most popular entertainers, but offstage he suffered greatly because he was an African American. He was not allowed to ride the elevator or eat in the dining rooms of the hotels where he stayed while traveling with his shows.

W. C. Fields, a famous comedian who worked with Bert, said he was "the funniest man I ever saw and the saddest man I ever knew." Although he became sick and exhausted, Bert Williams refused to stop working. He died in 1922 after collapsing during the performance of his new show, *Under the Bamboo Tree*.

MATTHEW HENSON

Matthew Henson

Matthew Henson was born on a farm in Maryland in 1866, one year after the end of the Civil War. When he was thirteen, he went to sea as a cabin boy on a sailing ship that was headed for China. After that adventure, he made many ocean voyages around the world, becoming an expert sailor. When he was twenty-two, Matthew met Robert Peary, a famous explorer, and took a trip with him to South America. From then on, the two men made many trips together, including several voyages to the Arctic, the region around the North Pole. Henson was a skilled boat and igloo builder, hunter and dog team driver, and spoke the Eskimo language.

One of Admiral Peary's goals was to stand on the North Pole, a spot where no explorer had ever been before. Finally, in April, 1909, he and Matthew Henson took another trip to the Arctic. They had almost reached their destination when Peary became too sick to walk and had to be pulled in a dog sled. Matthew Henson walked on ahead and set his feet on the North Pole, where he planted an American flag.

Although Henson, an African American, was the first man to reach the North Pole, most of the honors went to Admiral Peary. Henson was all but forgotten until many years later when, in 1944, the United States Congress awarded medals to all members of the historic expedition.

Madame C. J. Walker

The woman who would become Madame C. J. Walker was born on a cotton plantation in Delta, Louisiana, in 1867. She was named Sarah Breedlove. By the time she was seven years old, both of her parents had died. She went to live with her sister, and when she was only fourteen, she was married. Her husband died when she was twenty, and she was left alone with her little daughter, A'Lelia. Sarah moved with her daughter to St. Louis, Missouri, where she supported them both for eighteen years by doing laundry for other people.

In the early 1900s, she created a hair-conditioning lotion for African Americans. This was the first in a line of hair-care products that became very popular with black women. In 1905, Sarah and her daughter moved to Denver, Colorado. There she married a newspaperman named Charles Walker and began calling herself Madame C. J. Walker. Madame Walker opened a factory where she could manufacture her own hair products. She was able to offer jobs to thousands of African-American women around the country, who sold the products. She and her husband were divorced, and in 1916 she moved to New York and built a beautiful mansion on land overlooking the Hudson River.

When Madame C. J. Walker died at the age of fifty-one, she was a millionaire and the richest African-American woman in America. She left generous donations to many colleges and organizations, including the NAACP (National Association for the Advancement of Colored People).

W. C. Handy

W. C. Handy, who grew up to be known as the "Father of the Blues," was born in a log cabin in Florence, Alabama, in 1873. His parents named him William Christopher Handy, but he was always called "W. C." He loved music, and when he was a child he taught himself to play the cornet. In his teens, he joined a traveling musical show.

Handy was a factory worker and a teacher for a while, but in 1893, he returned to music and led a small band that played at the World's Fair in Chicago. From then on, he stayed with his musical career, and in 1905, in Memphis, Tennessee, he started a band that played the African-American tunes he had heard back home in Alabama. He began to compose "blues" pieces—music created by African Americans to express their deepest feelings.

In 1909, Handy wrote a campaign song for Edward H. Crump, who was running for mayor of Memphis. Three years later, he published the tune as "Memphis Blues." It was the first written blues composition, and soon became a best seller. His next composition, "St. Louis Blues," is the one he is most famous for.

Handy moved to New York City to be closer to the music business, ran his own publishing company for a time, and remained devoted to the blues for the rest of his life.

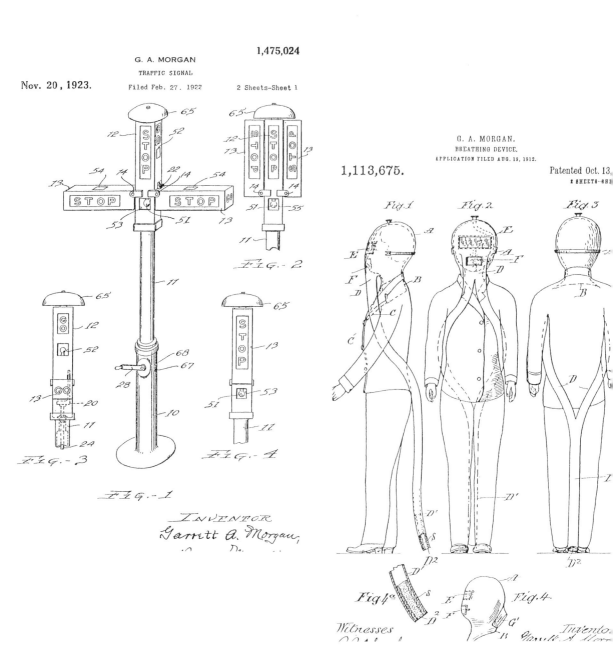

D<small>RAWINGS FOR</small> G<small>ARRETT</small> M<small>ORGAN'S INVENTIONS</small>

First to invent the automatic traffic light and the gas mask

Garrett A. Morgan

Garrett A. Morgan, who was to become a world-famous inventor, was born in 1875 on a farm in Paris, Kentucky. Not long after he finished elementary school, Garrett left home and moved to Cleveland, Ohio. He worked repairing sewing machines and later opened a tailor shop. While he was trying to make a special oil for his sewing machine needles to help them move more smoothly, he accidentally discovered a lotion that could be used to straighten curly hair. He sold it as the G. A. Morgan Hair Refining Cream.

In 1912, Garrett Morgan came up with a very important invention that he called a "breathing device." It had a hood that fitted over people's heads and helped them breathe when the air was not safe. Four years later, there was a huge explosion in a tunnel under Lake Erie, near Cleveland. The men who were working there were trapped. Garrett and his brother put on the breathing devices, went into the smoke-filled tunnel, and pulled the workers to safety. The invention later became the gas mask, which is still used today.

Garrett Morgan also is famous for another invention, the automatic traffic light. One day on a busy street corner he saw an accident between a car and a horse-drawn carriage. He later created a device that would help do away with such accidents. The traffic light he invented, with its "stop" and "go" signals, is used to control traffic in towns and cities all over the country. Like Morgan's other invention, the gas mask, the traffic light has saved many lives.

Paul Williams

Some of the most beautiful houses and buildings in and around Los Angeles, California, were designed by an African-American architect named Paul Revere Williams. He was born in that city in 1894 on downtown Olvera Street, where his parents owned a grocery store. By the time Paul was four years old, both of his parents had died of tuberculosis. He was adopted by a loving family and had a happy childhood. When he reached high school, he knew he wanted to be an architect, but a teacher told him it was a bad idea because he was an African American and wouldn't be able to find enough clients.

Paul Williams ignored that advice and pursued his dream. In his early twenties, he worked for several architects and studied at the University of Southern California. He opened his own office in 1922, and a year later was admitted to an important organization called the American Institute of Architects as its first African-American member.

Since there were so few black architects, Williams had to work hard to be accepted, but because of his talent and skill he eventually attracted many clients. He designed hundreds of homes in wealthy areas of Los Angeles. He became known as the "architect to the stars," since Frank Sinatra, Lucille Ball, and many other Hollywood entertainers were his clients. He also designed numerous other buildings, including several in the African-American community.

Carter G. Woodson

Carter G. Woodson was born in 1875 in Virginia to parents who were slaves. After the Civil War, when his parents were freed, they raised their nine children on a small farm. The Woodsons worked hard to care for their family, and they made sure to teach their children the importance of education. Carter was the youngest boy, and quite sickly, so his mother gave him special attention.

When he was a teenager, Carter's family moved to West Virginia, where he got a job as a coal miner. Because he had to work to help earn money for his family, Carter wasn't able to go to high school until he was twenty years old. A brilliant student, he graduated in only two years, and went on to earn degrees from three colleges, including Harvard University. He never lost his faith in the value of education.

When Carter Woodson became a schoolteacher in Washington, D. C., he saw that his students knew very little about the contributions made by African Americans to the history and culture of their country. He decided to devote the rest of his life to spreading information about the achievements of black Americans. In 1926, Carter Woodson created Negro History Week, which would be celebrated every February to honor the accomplishments of African Americans. In 1976, this celebration was extended to last for the entire month of February, and called Black History Month. Today it is known as African-American History Month.

BESSIE COLEMAN

Bessie Coleman

When she was a child in Atlanta, Texas, where she was born in 1893, Bessie Coleman was a hard worker. She picked cotton and did laundry to help her mother meet the family's expenses. After she finished high school, Bessie went to live with her brother in Chicago, Illinois. She attended beauty school and got a job as a manicurist, doing people's nails.

For years, Bessie had been interested in flying. She read every book she could find on aviation. Finally, she decided to apply to flying school. But schools in the United States would not accept her because she was a woman and an African American.

A friend told Bessie that she might be able to find someone to teach her to fly if she went to another country. She saved her money, traveled to Europe, and was accepted at a flying school in France. She took lessons from French and German aviators. In 1921, she became the first African-American woman in the world to earn a pilot's license.

Bessie Coleman returned to the United States and toured the country, appearing in air shows where she performed daring stunts. She also went to schools and churches to talk about airplanes and flying.

Bessie's goal was to earn enough money to open a flying school for African Americans. However, in 1926, during an air show in Jacksonville, Florida, her plane went into a nose dive and crashed, and she was killed. Bessie Coleman did not live to realize her dream, but she is still remembered as "Brave Bessie," the first African-American woman pilot.

Garland Anderson

When Garland Anderson wrote his play, *Appearances*, he was working as a bellhop in a busy hotel in San Francisco, California. He had never even taken playwrighting lessons. In fact, he had only attended school for four years. When Garland was eleven, his mother died and he ran away from home. He educated himself by reading the Bible and studying other books on his own. His play, *Appearances*, was really about his own life. It was the story of a bellhop who believes he can accomplish anything if he has faith in himself.

Garland Anderson was determined to have *Appearances* produced on the stage in New York City. He drove all the way across the country from California to City Hall in New York City. Everybody who saw his car could read the banner he had tied to its side. The banner read: "San Francisco to New York for New York Production 'Appearances' by Garland Anderson The Black San Francisco Bellhop Playwright."

Anderson tried to convince many different people to produce his play on Broadway. He even invited the governor of New York to hear it read, and later went to Washington, D.C., to get the support of President Calvin Coolidge. Finally, all his efforts paid off and on October 13, 1925, *Appearances* opened at the Frolic Theatre on Broadway. It was the first full-length play by an African American to appear on Broadway. The play didn't get much attention and only ran for twenty-three performances. After seeing his dream come true, Garland Anderson returned to California and became a minister.

GARLAND ANDERSON

William Grant Still

William Grant Still was born in 1895 in Mississippi, where both of his parents were teachers. His father, who also played the cornet in a band, died when William was only three months old. While he was growing up, William heard a lot of music in his home. His grandmother sang spirituals and his stepfather played recordings of operas. William took violin lessons when he was a child, but he did not expect to become a professional musician. Instead, when he entered Wilberforce University in Ohio, he planned to major in science and study to be a doctor. But soon he started directing the college band and writing his own musical compositions. He decided he wanted to be a composer and left college. He played the violin in dance bands and shows until he was twenty-one. Then, with some money his father had left him in his will, William went to Oberlin College to study music.

When World War I started, William left school and joined the navy, where he sometimes played his violin for the white officers. After the war, he went to New York City to continue his study of music. He started composing concert pieces, using the influences of African-American music—spirituals, blues, and jazz—and in 1931 the Rochester Philharmonic performed his *Afro-American Symphony*. It was the first time a symphony orchestra had played a work by an African-American composer.

William Grant Still continued to make history in the world of con-

WILLIAM GRANT STILL

cert music. In 1935, he became the first African American to conduct a major symphony orchestra when he led the Los Angeles Philharmonic. And his opera, *Troubled Island*, was the first by an African-American composer to be performed by a leading opera company, the New York City Opera, in 1949.

Mary McLeod Bethune

Many members of Mary McLeod Bethune's family were slaves before the Civil War. By the time she was born in 1875, her parents had been freed and owned a farm in Mayesville, South Carolina. Mary wasn't able to start school until she was eleven years old, when an elementary school finally opened five miles from her home. She was so eager to learn that she walked back and forth every day. She went on to graduate from a private school for African-American girls in North Carolina and a Bible college in Chicago. She wanted to become a missionary and go to other countries to teach religion, but she was told there were no missionary jobs for African Americans.

Mary McLead Bethune then turned her attention to teaching, and taught for several years in southern schools. In 1904, when she was living in Daytona Beach, Florida, she decided to open her own school. She rented a small shabby house near the city dump, made desks out of old packing crates, and started her first class. Her students were five little girls and her own son.

Before long she decided to buy the nearby land and build a larger school. To help raise money, she and her students baked sweet potato pies and sold them to railroad workers. She was able to create a school that grew into an outstanding four-year college called Bethune-Cookman College.

Mary McLeod Bethune devoted herself to improving the lives of African Americans. In 1935, she started the National Council of Col-

MARY McLEOD BETHUNE

ored Women, an organization that worked to increase opportunities for black women. One year later, she became the first African-American woman to head a federal office when President Franklin D. Roosevelt appointed her director of the Office of Negro Affairs of the National Youth Administration.

Thomas A. Dorsey

Thomas A. Dorsey, who has been called "the father of gospel music," was born in 1899 in Villa Rica, Georgia, the son of a country preacher. His first piano teacher was his mother, Etta. By the time he was eight years old, he was able to play the pump organ in churches where his father preached his sermons. When he was a little older, he walked four miles a day four days a week to take piano lessons.

Thomas left Georgia for Chicago, Illinois, where he entered college to study music. He started playing a special kind of music called the "blues"—music that African Americans had created to express their feelings. Known as "Georgia Tom," Dorsey often performed blues piano in nightclubs.

Thomas Dorsey changed his life after he went to a National Baptist Convention and heard a choir sing a spiritual—a religious song—called "I Do, Don't You?" He decided to leave popular music and devote himself to writing spirituals. His songs combined religious music and the blues. He called them gospel songs. His best-known song, "Take My Hand, Precious Lord," was written after the death of his wife and child.

Thomas Dorsey founded the world's first gospel choir in 1931, at a Baptist church in Chicago, and started the first gospel publishing company a year later. At the time of his death at the age of ninety-three, Thomas Dorsey had written more than 1,000 gospel songs.

First African American to have a painting in the White House

Henry Ossawa Tanner

In December, 1996, a painting by an African-American artist was hung in the White House in Washington, D.C. for the first time. The name of the painting is *Sand Dunes at Sunset, Atlantic City*, and the artist is Henry Ossawa Tanner.

When Henry Ossawa Tanner was born in Pittsburgh, Pennsylvania, in 1859, his mother was a schoolteacher who had once been a slave, and his father was a minister in the African Methodist Episcopal Church who later became a bishop. His parents hoped that he, too, would study to be a minister. However, one day when Henry was about twelve years old, he was walking with his father in a park where he saw an artist at work. Henry went home and started making his own drawings. Soon he decided he wanted to become a painter, and enrolled in an art school in Philadelphia.

After college, Tanner worked for a time as a photographer, traveling through North Carolina where he took pictures and made drawings of people who lived in the back country. From these sketches, he produced one of his most famous paintings, *Banjo Lesson*, which shows an elderly man teaching a child to play the banjo.

Tanner traveled to Paris, France, where he spent most of the rest of his life. For several years, he painted the everyday activities of ordinary African Americans. Later, he concentrated on religious paintings. One of his most famous is called *Daniel in the Lion's Den*.

First to set up a blood bank

Charles Drew

As a student at Dunbar High School in Washington, D.C., where he was born in 1904, Charles Drew was an outstanding athlete, starring in several sports. He was also an excellent student, and went on to attend Amherst College. He dreamed of becoming a doctor, but did not have enough money for medical school, so after graduating from Amherst he got a job teaching biology and chemistry at Morgan State College. Two years later, he was able to enroll in McGill University Medical School, in Montreal, Canada. He earned a Doctor of Medicine degree and returned to Washington to teach at Howard University.

Dr. Drew began to study ways that blood could be stored, so that it could be used later in transfusions for patients who needed extra blood. While doing research at Columbia University in New York City, he developed a way to separate plasma, the liquid part of blood, and store it until it was needed. In 1939, he set up the country's first blood plasma bank at Columbia-Presbyterian Medical Center.

Two years later, he became head of an American Red Cross program to collect and store blood to be used for soldiers injured in World War II. However, the armed forces at first refused to take blood from African-American donors. Later, it was accepted, but kept separate from that of whites. Dr. Drew left the Red Cross, saying that there was no difference between the blood of African Americans and whites. His work was responsible for saving many lives.

Jesse Owens

This record-breaking track star was born in 1913 in a small Alabama town. His parents, who were poor cotton farmers, named him James Cleveland Owens. His family called him J.C., which his teachers and friends later changed to Jesse. While he was still in elementary school, Jesse dreamed of someday going to college. To help him reach his goal, his parents moved to Cleveland, Ohio, where they could find better jobs. In Cleveland, Jesse's gym teacher started training him for the high school track team. He joined the team and began breaking many records. He continued his track career in college, at Ohio State University, where he once set three world records in less than an hour.

In 1936, Jesse Owens was chosen to compete in the Olympic Games, which were being held in Berlin, Germany. Adolf Hitler, who was the dictator of Nazi Germany at that time, wanted to prove that the Germans were the "master race" and could win all the contests. But Jesse Owens, an African American, proved Hitler wrong by winning four gold medals. It was the first time any athlete had won four gold medals in a single Olympics.

When Owens returned to the United States, he was given a big parade in New York City. He then began an ordinary life, working at several different jobs to support his family. He died in 1980, but his victory at the Olympic Games in Germany will never be forgotten.

Benjamin O. Davis, Sr.

Benjamin O. Davis grew up in Washington, D.C., where he was born in 1877. He attended Howard University for one year and, when he was twenty-one years old, he enlisted in the army. This was the beginning of a military career that would last for fifty years. He served in the Spanish-American War, World War I, and World War II, receiving many honors, including the Bronze Star and the Distinguished Service Medal. Benjamin Davis made history in 1940 when President Franklin Roosevelt appointed him a brigadier general, making him the country's first African-American general.

During World War II, many of Davis's assignments had to do with racial issues. At that time, the armed forces were segregated. White and black soldiers were not allowed to live or fight together. Despite this rule, tens of thousands of African Americans fought and died for their country. General Davis worked hard to convince the armed forces to end segregation, and in 1948, President Harry Truman announced that black and white soldiers and sailors would be treated equally.

While Benjamin Davis, Sr., was becoming an important army general, his son, Benjamin Davis, Jr., was following in his footsteps. The younger Davis graduated from the U.S. Military Academy at West Point in 1936, and in World War II he led a famous group of African-American fighter pilots called the Tuskegee Airmen. In 1954, Benjamin Davis, Jr., was made the first African-American brigadier general in the air force.

Brig. Gen. Benjamin O. Davis, Sr.

Hattie McDaniel

Hattie McDaniel was born in 1895 in Wichita, Kansas, where her father was a Baptist preacher and her mother sang in the church choir. When she was six years old, her family settled in Denver, Colorado. It was there, when she was fifteen, that she won a gold medal for reciting a poem called "Convict Joe." She was such a talented actress that her father let her join a traveling stage show that he had formed. She later became a singer with a popular orchestra in Denver, and it is said that she was the first African-American woman to sing on the radio.

In 1931, she went to Hollywood, where she had to work as a maid until she started getting regular roles in movies. She appeared on screen for the first time in 1932 in a movie called *The Golden West*, and was featured in more than fifty films. Even in the movies, though, Hattie McDaniel was usually given the role of a maid. She was such a good actress, however, that audiences always remembered her. When some people criticized her for the parts that she played, McDaniel said, "It's better to play a maid than to be one."

Hattie McDaniel's talent was rewarded when she was given an Academy Award as Best Supporting Actress for her performance as Mammy in the 1939 hit movie, *Gone With the Wind*. She was the first African American to win an Oscar.

Dorie Miller

Dorie Miller was born in 1919 on his parents' small farm outside of Waco, Texas. He spent a few years in elementary school, and then left to go to work on the family farm. In 1940, Dorie decided to enlist in the navy. In those days, African-American sailors were only allowed to do such jobs as cook and serve food and clean up the kitchen. They were given no training in the use of guns.

When the United States entered World War II in December, 1941, Dorie Miller was assigned to a ship called the *West Virginia*, which was docked at Pearl Harbor, a U.S. naval base in Hawaii. On the Sunday morning of December 7, 1941, Miller was surprised to hear airplanes roaring overhead. He ran on deck and saw Japanese planes attacking the ship with torpedoes. Miller rushed to a machine gun and began firing. Before he had to leave the ship, he had shot down four enemy planes.

Dorie Miller's brave actions made him the first American hero of World War II. Six months later, he was awarded the Navy Cross, a medal given to those who show great courage. Dorie Miller was then assigned to another warship, where he was trained to be a cook. In 1943, his ship was hit by a Japanese torpedo and sank with all the sailors still on it. Dorie Miller was twenty-four years old when he died. Thirty years later a navy warship, the U.S.S. *Miller*, was named in his honor.

Satchel Paige

Satchel Paige

When this famous baseball player was born in Mobile, Alabama, his parents named him Leroy Paige. He always said he was born in 1906, but some people think it may have been earlier. When Leroy was seven years old, he began earning money at the railroad station by carrying suitcases and smaller bags called satchels. People say that he could dangle several satchels at a time from a long pole that he carried. The other children called him "satchel tree." This was later shortened to Satchel and that name stayed with him.

Satchel also had a job cleaning up the town ball park, and it was there that he became interested in baseball. He could not afford a ball, so he practiced by pitching rocks. When he was twelve, he was caught stealing some cheap rings. He was sent to a reform school where the coach helped him learn the game of baseball and develop his pitching style. In 1924, he was signed up as a pitcher for the Mobile Tigers baseball team. For the next twenty-four years, he played for several different African-American teams in what was called the Negro Leagues. At that time, black players were not allowed to play on white teams.

In 1947, a ballplayer named Jackie Robinson became the first African American to play in the major leagues since the early days of baseball. One year later, Satchel Paige was signed by the Cleveland Indians, a major league team. Many fans thought that Satchel Paige was the greatest pitcher in the history of baseball. One of his special pitches was called the "bee ball." It went by so fast that you could hear it buzz, but you couldn't see it.

Wesley A. Brown

The United States Naval Academy opened in Annapolis, Maryland, in 1845 as a school for the training of navy officers. During the Academy's first ninety-five years, only five African Americans were admitted. All left the school or were dismissed after they were told that they had poor grades or didn't behave well. When the last two African Americans left the Academy in the 1930s, black organizations charged that the young men had been discriminated against because of their race.

Then, in June, 1945, a young African American named Wesley A. Brown, who came from Washington, D.C., was chosen to attend the Naval Academy. Wesley had been an excellent student at Dunbar High School in Washington. He was active in German, chess, and photography clubs, and participated in tennis and track. His teachers encouraged him to follow a career in the military service.

Wesley Brown's first year at the Naval Academy was very difficult. Many of his classmates were unkind to him because he was an African American, and his teachers often scolded him. After he had been there a while, though, the other students changed their attitude toward him, and his instructors also started treating him better.

No matter how people behaved toward him, Wesley never gave up, and in June, 1949, he became the first African American to graduate from the U.S. Naval Academy. He went on to serve in the navy for twenty years, and then became a professor at Howard University. When he retired, he held the rank of lieutenant commander. He often returned

LT. COMDR. WESLEY A. BROWN

to the Academy to give words of encouragement to African-American students.

Alice Coachman

When Alice Coachman broke a world high jump record by leaping five feet, six and one-quarter inches at the 1948 Olympic Games, she became the first African-American woman to win a gold medal. Alice had been winning track and field competitions for almost ten years. She became interested in the high jump when she attended a boys' track and field meet in Albany, Georgia, where she was born in 1921. At first, Alice practiced the sport by jumping over a rope tied between two trees. Then, when she was sixteen, she entered a track meet at Tuskegee Institute in Alabama. The coach was impressed by her skill, and she became a student at Tuskegee, winning many events for the school. She continued to win high jump titles at Albany State College, where she studied home economics and science.

In 1948, Alice Coachman won a place on the track and field team for the Summer Olympics, which were being held in London, England. Before a crowd of 65,000 spectators, she beat her closest rival and won a gold medal for setting a new Olympic high jump record. When she returned home, she was greeted with parades in her honor. She chose a career as a physical education teacher, got married, and had a son and daughter who were both talented athletes.

Ralph Ellison

Ralph Ellison was just three years old when his father was killed in an accident in their home town of Oklahoma City, where Ralph had been born in 1914. His father had supported the family by selling ice and coal. Now his mother had to earn money by cleaning houses. Ralph loved to read when he was a child, but his first ambition was to be a musician. He started playing the trumpet at the age of eight, and in high school he took music lessons and played in the band. After high school, he entered Tuskegee Institute in Alabama to study music. At the end of his junior year, he traveled to New York City, planning to find a job to help pay for his college expenses.

Ellison never returned to Alabama. Soon after his arrival in New York, he met the African-American writers, Langston Hughes and Richard Wright. They encouraged him to develop his talent for creative writing. At first, he wrote short stories and essays. Then, at the end of World War II, after serving as a cook in the Merchant Marine, Ellison started work on a novel. One day, sitting before a typewriter, he wrote, "I am an invisible man." These words became the opening line of his novel, *Invisible Man*, which was published seven years later, in 1952. The book told the story of a young black man's struggle to find his identity in a white world. The National Book Award, an important prize for writers, was awarded to Ralph Ellison for *Invisible Man*, and his novel is now considered one of the great books of the twentieth century.

First African American to win the Nobel Peace Prize

Ralph Bunche

Ralph Bunche was one of America's most outstanding diplomats. Born in Detroit, Michigan, in 1904, Ralph was abandoned by his father when a child. He was a teenager when his mother died and he went to live with his grandmother in Los Angeles, California. There he graduated first in his high school class.

As a student at the University of California at Los Angeles, he was active in sports and on the debating team, and he again graduated first in his class. Helped by a scholarship from a group of African-American women, he entered Harvard University in 1927 and graduated with a master's degree in political science. He earned the title of Dr. Ralph Bunche in 1934 when he was awarded a Ph.D. in political science from Harvard.

In 1941, Ralph Bunche went to work for a government agency, and in 1944 he became the first African American in the State Department. He became increasingly involved in political affairs throughout the world. In 1947, he arranged a cease-fire in the war between the Arabs and Israelis. This accomplishment earned him the Nobel Peace Prize in 1950. He was the first African American to win this award.

In 1967, Ralph Bunche was appointed Undersecretary General of the United Nations, the highest position ever held by an American at the UN. He held this post until ill health forced him to retire in 1971. He died several months later.

Gwendolyn Brooks

Gwendolyn Brooks was born in 1917 in Topeka, Kansas, but grew up in the city of Chicago, Illinois, where she spent her life. She had a happy childhood living in African-American neighborhoods with her parents and her younger brother, Raymond. "I had always felt that to be black was good," she wrote in her autobiography. When Gwendolyn was a child, her father, David Brooks, worked as a janitor, although he had spent a year in college, hoping to become a doctor. Her mother, Keziah, had been a fifth-grade teacher.

Gwendolyn began to write poetry when she was seven years old, and both of her parents encouraged her interest in writing. When she was older, her mother took her to meet the famous African-American poet Langston Hughes, who became her friend and teacher.

Gwendolyn graduated from a junior college and later married a writer she had met in a poetry workshop. They had two children. She continued to write poetry, and in 1950 she was awarded a Pulitzer Prize for her collection of poems titled *Annie Allen*. She was the first African American to win this important prize.

Gwendolyn Brooks went on to publish several more books and win many awards for her writing. She has spent much of her time giving help to beginning poets, and has taught schoolchildren, teenage gang members, prisoners, and homeless people.

THE CIVIL RIGHTS MOVEMENT

In December, 1955, when an African-American woman named Rosa Parks refused to give up her seat to a white passenger on a bus in Montgomery, Alabama, she was arrested and taken to the city jail. During that time in the South, there were rules and regulations, called "Jim Crow" laws, that applied only to black people. In most cities in the South, African Americans were forced to sit in the back of buses and give up their seats to whites if they were asked. Rosa Parks did not realize that her actions on that December day were the first step in what would be called the Civil Rights Movement.

After Rosa Parks's arrest, black ministers and leaders in Montgomery met to organize a boycott of the city's buses. They wanted all African Americans to refuse to ride on the buses, which meant that the city would lose a great deal of money. A twenty-six-year-old minister, the Reverend Martin Luther King, Jr., was chosen to be their leader. The bus boycott lasted for more than a year, and in 1956, the United States Supreme Court—the highest court in the country—said that Alabama's buses could no longer be segregated. African-American people could sit wherever they wanted.

This victory encouraged others to try to change laws that did not give African Americans equal rights and opportunities. To attract attention to these efforts, numerous marches and demonstrations were held. Some were peaceful and others ended in violence and death. The Civil

Rights Movement brought great changes to American society. Many people, both black and white, worked together to end unfair treatment in the areas of housing, education, and voting rights. Because of these efforts, African Americans gained opportunities in many areas, from entertainment and sports to medicine, government, and the arts.

First African-American principal dancer in a ballet company

Arthur Mitchell

Arthur Mitchell was born in New York City in 1934. When he was ten years old, he took his first tap-dance lessons. These early classes led to a career that made him one of the country's most acclaimed dancers.

Mitchell studied modern dance at the High School of Performing Arts. He was still in high school when he performed in an opera in Paris, France, and was honored at his graduation when he became the first male student to win the school's dance award. He was given a scholarship to study at the School of American Ballet, and soon his exciting style led to performances with several dance companies.

In 1955, Arthur Mitchell joined one of the most outstanding companies of all, the New York City Ballet. He was given a leading role in a ballet called *Western Symphony*, becoming the first African-American principal dancer in an American ballet company.

Mitchell was deeply affected by the assassination of Dr. Martin Luther King, Jr., in 1968, and decided to do something positive in response. As a way to help young African Americans develop their talent in dance, he opened a small ballet school in the basement of a church in the Harlem neighborhood of New York City. The school grew into a professional African-American dance company called the Dance Theatre of Harlem, which gave its first public performance in 1971.

Marian Anderson

When Marian Anderson was only six years old, she began singing in the choir of her church in Philadelphia, Pennsylvania, where she was born in 1897. The choir director was surprised that the little girl could sing all four parts of the hymns. By the time she was in her teens, the members of her church were so impressed by her beautiful voice that they collected money to pay for her singing lessons. Marian's father had died when she was a child, and her mother took in laundry to support the family. She couldn't afford any extra expenses.

Marian gave her first concerts in Philadelphia, and in 1925 she won first prize in a voice competition in New York City and started performing there. In 1930, when her singing engagements began to dwindle, she went to Europe in search of more opportunities. She gave concerts in several countries, and they were great successes. A famous conductor, Arturo Toscanini, said, "A voice like hers comes once in a century."

Marian Anderson returned to New York in 1935, and started giving concerts all over the United States. Critics said she was one of the greatest singers of the time. However, in spite of all the praise she received, Anderson sometimes experienced insults because of her race. In 1939, a women's organization kept her from singing in Constitution Hall in Washington, D.C. The President's wife, Eleanor Roosevelt, was so upset by this incident that she sponsored an Easter Sunday concert on the grounds of the Lincoln Memorial, where Anderson sang for an audience of 75,000 people. Finally, in January, 1955, Mar-

MARIAN ANDERSON

ian Anderson was asked to sing at the famous Metropolitan Opera House in New York City. She was the first African American to sing on that stage.

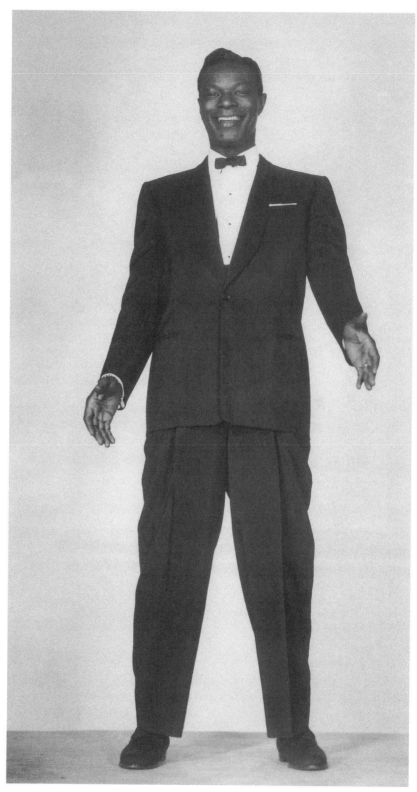

NAT KING COLE

Nat King Cole

Nathaniel Adams Cole was born in Montgomery, Alabama, in 1919 and was two years old when his family moved to Chicago. His father was the pastor of a Baptist church, where young Nathaniel sang and played the organ. His parents encouraged his musical talent and Nathaniel became an excellent piano player. While still in high school, he formed his own band. After graduation, he struggled to succeed as a musician, playing the piano in clubs and putting together several different small bands. In the 1940s, using the name Nat King Cole, he formed the King Cole Trio, which became very popular.

In 1944, the King Cole Trio recorded its first hit song, "Straighten Up and Fly Right," with Nat King Cole singing. Four years later, a record of Cole singing a song called "Nature Boy" was a big success. He became one of the first African-American singers to be popular with both black and white music lovers. His records were big sellers and he was often a guest on television shows.

In November, 1956, Nat King Cole appeared for the first time on NBC as host of his own weekly television program. He was the first African American to host a network television series. However, even though he was very popular, the show was unable to find a regular sponsor. It was cancelled after just one year. Nat was hurt and disappointed. He was angry with advertising agencies for not trying hard enough to sell his show to sponsors. In 1965, he died of lung cancer at the age of forty-six. His daughter, Natalie Cole, became a successful pop singer.

Lorraine Hansberry

When Lorraine Hansberry's play, *Raisin in the Sun*, opened on Broadway in New York City in March, 1959, she became famous overnight. Hansberry had worked and studied hard during the years that led to her success. She was born in 1930 in Chicago, Illinois, where her parents were active in groups that supported equal opportunities for African Americans. Her interest in the theater began when she was in high school, and she later studied art and stage design at the University of Wisconsin. She was strongly affected by a college production of a play by Sean O'Casey that portrayed the suffering of the Irish people. Her memories of that production inspired her when she later wrote about the struggles of an African-American family in her own play.

Hansberry left college after two years and moved to New York City, where she worked at a variety of jobs and wrote poems, short stories, and plays. Finally, calling upon her memories of the hard-working African-American people she'd known in Chicago, she wrote *Raisin in the Sun*. It opened in a Broadway theater in March, 1959, making Hansberry the first African-American woman to write a play produced on Broadway. The play, a great success, was later made into a movie. Hansberry became ill with cancer in 1963, but never stopped writing until her death two years later.

Mal Goode

Malvin R. Goode, who was known as Mal, got his start as a news reporter for a radio station in Pittsburgh, Pennsylvania, where he attended college. Goode was born in 1908 in White Plains, Virginia, and later moved to Pennsylvania. During high school and college, he worked as a laborer in the steel mills, a job he kept for five years after graduating from the University of Pittsburgh.

In 1948, Goode's journalism career began when he was hired as a reporter for an African-American newspaper called the *Pittsburgh Courier*. A year later, he joined a local radio station, doing a fifteen-minute news show twice a week. In 1950, he was hired by radio station WHOD, becoming news director two years later. Broadcasting from WHOD, he and his sister, Mary Dee, had the only brother-and-sister team on radio for six years.

In 1962, Mal Goode was hired by ABC-TV after the baseball player, Jackie Robinson, told an official that the only African Americans he'd seen at that television station were the cleaning woman and the doorman. Goode, the first African-American network television reporter, was assigned to cover the United Nations. During his eleven years at ABC, Mal Goode reported on many important stories, including the Cuban missile crisis, national political conventions, and many events of the Civil Rights Movement.

WILT CHAMBERLAIN

First basketball player to score 100 points in a single game

Wilt Chamberlain

Wilton Norman Chamberlain was born in Philadelphia, Pennsylvania, in 1936. He was one of nine children. His father was a custodian and his mother earned money by cleaning houses. Always large for his age, Wilt grew to be 7 feet 2 inches tall. His nickname was "Wilt the Stilt." He was an outstanding athlete in high school and participated in several sports, including track and field, football, and basketball.

Wilt was asked to join professional teams while he was still in high school, but he decided to go to college instead. He entered the University of Kansas, where he led the basketball team to the national college finals. He left college before his senior year to play with a popular basketball team called the Harlem Globetrotters.

In 1959, Wilt Chamberlain signed up to play with the Philadelphia Warriors. In the 1961–62 season, he gained fame by becoming the first basketball player ever to score 100 points in a single game. Wilt was later traded to the Philadelphia 76ers and led them to a championship in the 1966–67 season. In February, 1972, while playing for the Los Angeles Lakers, he broke another record. He became the first player in the National Basketball Association to score a total of 30,000 points.

After he retired from basketball, Wilt Chamberlain started a volleyball organization, sponsored track and field meets, and appeared in movies and television commercials. In 1979, this legendary star of the courts was elected to the Basketball Hall of Fame.

Sidney Poitier

Sidney Poitier worked at any job he could find before he finally was able to support himself as an actor. The youngest of eight children, Sidney was born in Miami, Florida, in 1927, but grew up on Cat Island in the Bahamas, a country in the West Indies. When he was fifteen, he had to leave school to work on his parents' tomato farm. Three years later, he moved to New York City, where he worked as a dock-hand, dishwasher, and chicken plucker while studying to be an actor.

Poitier applied for a job with the American Negro Theatre, but was rejected because of his West Indian accent. For the next six months, he practiced speaking along with the radio and then reapplied. This time the theater company took him in.

Poitier acted on the New York stage in a number of plays, but his big break came in 1950 when he was given the leading role of a young doctor in the movie, *No Way Out*. He stayed in Hollywood to star in such films as *Cry, the Beloved Country, Blackboard Jungle*, and *The Defiant Ones*. Back in New York in 1959, Sidney Poitier appeared on Broadway in *Raisin in the Sun*, written by the African-American play-wright, Lorraine Hansberry. Two years later, he repeated the role in the movie version of the play. Then, in 1963, Sidney Poitier won an Oscar for his performance in *Lilies of the Field*, becoming the first African-American man to receive an Academy Award.

Thurgood Marshall

When he tried to attend law school in Baltimore, Maryland, where he was born in 1908, Thurgood Marshall was kept out because he was an African American. In later years, this great-grandson of a slave would be considered one of the greatest lawyers of the twentieth century.

In grade school and high school, Marshall was full of mischief. As punishment for misbehavior, one of his teachers made students read parts of the U.S. Constitution. By the time the year was over, Marshall had read the whole thing. After high school, Marshall attended an African-American college in Pennsylvania called Lincoln University, where he waited on tables to help pay his expenses.

Thurgood Marshall was rejected by the all-white University of Maryland law school, and enrolled in Howard University, an African-American school in Washington, D.C. To pay his entrance fee, his mother borrowed money in exchange for her wedding and engagement rings. He paid her back by graduating first in his class.

When he became a lawyer, Marshall brought a lawsuit against the University of Maryland, and a judge ordered the school to end segregation and admit black students. But his greatest victory came in 1954 when he won a case that forced all public schools to admit students of all races. Over the years, Thurgood Marshall won many other important cases. In 1967, he made history when he became the first African-American justice on the United States Supreme Court—the highest court in the country.

Arthur Ashe

Arthur Ashe was born in July, 1943, and began playing tennis in his hometown of Richmond, Virginia, when he was ten years old. Arthur's mother died when he was six, and as he grew up he learned good manners and a positive attitude from his father, Arthur Ashe, Sr. At that time, black and white children in Richmond could not use the same playgrounds. Arthur learned tennis in a playground for African Americans where his father was a supervisor.

When Arthur was seventeen, in 1960, he won his first national tennis title, the National Indoor Junior Tennis Championship. One year later, he became the first African-American member of the United States Junior Davis Cup Team, a group of leading young tennis players, and he was awarded a scholarship to the University of California.

Sometimes Arthur Ashe was not allowed to play in tournaments because of his race, but still he went on to achieve many firsts in tennis. He was the first African American to win the U.S. Open, in 1968, the first to win men's singles at Wimbledon in England, in 1975, and the first African-American man inducted into the International Tennis Hall of Fame.

Throughout his tennis career, Arthur Ashe was a fighter for civil rights, speaking out against the unfair treatment of African Americans. In 1979, he suffered a heart attack and had to have two heart operations. He later learned that he had contracted the HIV virus from blood transfusions during one of the operations. At that time, blood used in transfusions was not tested the way it is now. After he announced in 1992 that he had the virus that causes AIDS, he became

ARTHUR ASHE

active in efforts to combat the disease. On February 6, 1993, at the age of forty-nine, Arthur Ashe died of AIDS, leaving behind his wife, Jeanne, a photographer, and their daughter, Camera.

Shirley Chisholm

Shirley Chisholm was born in Brooklyn, New York, in 1924, but she spent her childhood with her family on the island of Barbados in the West Indies. After returning to New York, she attended Brooklyn College and Columbia University to prepare for a career as a teacher. Later, when she wrote her autobiography, *Unbought and Unbossed*, she explained that she became a teacher because "there was no other road open to a young black woman." Law, medicine, and nursing were too expensive, she said, "and few schools would admit black men, much less a woman."

Shirley Chisholm became active in politics and was elected to the New York State Assembly in 1964. Four years later, running as a Democrat from Brooklyn, she became the first African-American woman to be elected to the United States Congress.

In 1972, she announced that she would seek the Democratic Party nomination as a candidate for President of the United States. It was the first time an African-American woman had run for the presidential nomination of a major political party. Although she did not win the nomination, Shirley Chisholm spoke out for more programs for poor people and equal rights for minorities and women. She said she hoped her campaign would help make it easier for other women and African Americans to run for president.

First African-American woman to host a national TV talk show

Oprah Winfrey

One of the most successful entertainers in America, Oprah Winfrey has worked hard to do her best. Born in Kosciusko, Mississippi, in 1954, she was raised by her grandmother until she was six. Then she went to Milwaukee, Wisconsin, to live with her mother, who earned a living by cleaning houses.

Oprah was a smart child with a talent for reciting poetry, and was often invited to perform at parties. But by the time she was a teenager, she had started to misbehave, so she was sent to stay with her father, who lived in Nashville, Tennessee. He made sure that she did well in school, and she won prizes for debating and making speeches. At sixteen, she won a college scholarship in a speech contest.

Oprah Winfrey graduated from Tennessee State University in 1976, and was hired as a reporter by a television station in Baltimore, Maryland. A year later, she was made co-host of a morning talk show, where she stayed until she went to Chicago as a talk-show host. She attracted such a wide audience that the program was named "The Oprah Winfrey Show," and soon it was seen around the country. Oprah also became an actress, starring in the movie *The Color Purple*. In 1988, she became the first African-American woman to form her own television and film production company, Harpo Productions, which has created several television dramas.

Moneta Sleet, Jr.

The photographer Moneta Sleet, Jr., met Dr. Martin Luther King, Jr., in 1955, at the beginning of the Civil Rights Movement. Over the next thirteen years, he took hundreds of pictures of Dr. King and other civil rights leaders. He reached the peak of his career in 1968, when he won a Pulitzer Prize for a picture he took at Dr. King's funeral.

Moneta Sleet, who was born in Owensburg, Kentucky, in 1926, took his first pictures with a camera his parents gave him when he was a young boy. Although he studied business administration in college, Sleet later took a photography course and then taught for a year at a college in Maryland.

In 1950, Moneta Sleet earned a master's degree in journalism, and after a short time as a sports reporter for a New York City newspaper, he was hired as a staff photographer for a popular African-American magazine called *Our World*. Five years later, he went to work for *Ebony*, a leading black magazine. He spent his entire career there, traveling all over the world to take pictures of black leaders and celebrities, as well as ordinary people, especially children.

Sleet traveled to Sweden in 1964 to photograph Dr. King when he received the Nobel Peace Prize. Four years later, after the famed civil rights leader was assassinated, Sleet was chosen to take pictures at his funeral. The photograph that later appeared in newspapers through-out the country showed Dr. King's little daughter, Bernice, sadly resting her head in her mother's lap during the funeral service. For this picture, Moneta Sleet became the first African-American man to win

MONETA SLEET, JR.

a Pulitzer Prize. Sleet continued his successful career until October, 1996, when he died just a few months after photographing the Summer Olympics in Atlanta.

GUION S. BLUFORD

Guion S. Bluford

The African-American astronaut, Guion S. Bluford, Jr., has flown in space four times and has been a leader in the aerospace industry. He says that he owes his success to his parents. His father was a mechanical engineer and his mother was a schoolteacher who stressed the importance of education.

Guion was born in 1942 in Philadelphia, Pennsylvania. By the time he was in his early teens, he knew he wanted to be an engineer like his father and to specialize in the field of space exploration. He attended colleges and universities to learn all that he could.

Guion loved airplanes and learned to fly, earning his wings in 1965. He served in the United States Air Force for thirteen years and was a pilot in Vietnam, where he flew 144 combat missions. He also taught flying for five years at an air force base in Texas. In 1978, Bluford was accepted into the NASA astronaut program, where he was trained for his first mission. On August 30, 1983, he became the first African-American astronaut in space when he flew aboard the space shuttle *Challenger* on its night launch from the Kennedy Space Center in Florida.

Two years later, Bluford traveled into space again, spending seven days aboard the *Challenger* on the country's first spacelab mission, where he helped perform several experiments. He ended his space career by flying twice more, in 1991 and 1992, aboard the *Discovery*. In 1993, Bluford resigned from NASA and the air force and went to work for a private engineering company.

DR. BENJAMIN CARSON

Benjamin Carson

Dr. Benjamin Carson overcame many obstacles before achieving success as a surgeon. Born in 1951, he grew up in a poor neighborhood of Detroit, Michigan. Because his father left the family when Ben was eight years old, his mother had to work hard to support her two sons. She felt that education was very important and made the boys read at least two books a week and write a report on each.

Despite his mother's encouragement, Ben was not a good student in elementary school, but his grades improved as he grew older. By the time he graduated from high school, he was third in his class and had won a scholarship to Yale University. After graduating from Yale, he went on to attend the University of Michigan School of Medicine.

Dr. Benjamin Carson became a pediatric neurosurgeon—a doctor who treats the nervous system of children. In 1984, when he was thirty-three years old, Dr. Carson was appointed director of pediatric neurosurgery at Johns Hopkins University Hospital in Baltimore, Maryland. He was the youngest person ever to hold that position.

Dr. Carson has performed many operations that helped improve or save the lives of children, but he is best known for an operation performed in 1987. It was then that he led a medical team that, for the first time, successfully separated twins who were joined at the head. Although he is a busy neurosurgeon, Dr. Carson sets aside time to talk to schoolchildren. In one of his speeches, he said, "You don't have to be a brain surgeon to be a valuable person. You become valuable because of the knowledge that you have. And that doesn't mean you won't fail sometimes. The important thing is to keep trying."

Muhammad Ali

The boxer known as Muhammed Ali was born in 1942 in Louisville, Kentucky. His parents named him Cassius Marcellus Clay. As a youngster, he loved boxing, and he was only twelve when a Louisville policeman began training him as a fighter. He showed great talent and soon was one of the best amateur fighters in the country. He became a national amateur champion, and when he was eighteen years old, Clay won a gold medal in the heavyweight division at the Olympic Games in Rome, Italy. After he returned home, he decided to become a professional boxer.

In 1964, Cassius Clay won the heavyweight championship by defeating a fighter named Charles "Sonny" Liston, knocking him out in seven rounds. After the fight, he announced that he had joined a religious group called the Nation of Islam and had changed his name to Muhammad Ali. Three years later, in 1967, Ali took a stand and refused to go into the army. He said he was opposed to the Vietnam War because of his religious beliefs. Since he would not fight in the war, his heavyweight title was taken away from him and he did not box again until he was allowed to return to the sport in 1970.

Muhammad Ali began a comeback and in 1974 regained the championship by defeating George Foreman. He lost it again in 1978, but won it back that same year. Ali was known for his good-natured boasting and his poetic use of the English language. For most of his career, he could, as he said, "float like a butterfly, sting like a bee."

Aretha Franklin

The Rock and Roll Hall of Fame opened in 1986, and a year later admitted its first woman, the famed singer, Aretha Franklin. Born in 1942 in Memphis, Tennessee, Aretha Louise Franklin grew up in Detroit, Michigan, where her father was a minister. When Aretha was six years old, her mother left the family, and four years later she died. Her father, the Reverend C. L. Franklin, became the only parent to raise Aretha, her two sisters, and her two brothers.

As pastor of the New Bethel Baptist Church, the Reverend Franklin was famous for his sermons, which were sold on records. Aretha, a very shy child, met many gospel singers who came to visit her father, and they inspired her to become a singer, too. She sang her first solo in her father's church when she was twelve, and made her first gospel record two years later. By then she was traveling around the country, singing in churches with a gospel group.

In 1960, Aretha moved to New York City to try to make it as a singer. She was signed by Columbia Records, but wasn't allowed to sing the kind of blues music that she enjoyed the most. In 1966, she began to record with Atlantic Records, where she sang a special kind of African-American music called "soul." She became known as the "Queen of Soul," and won Grammy awards every year from 1967 to 1975. Aretha Franklin is still singing, and when she learned that she was the first woman to be in the Rock and Roll Hall of Fame, she said, "Well, the doors are now open, girls!"

African Americans Today

The achievements of African Americans today are the result of the sacrifices and struggles of those who came before them. Over the years, whites as well as blacks have joined in efforts to win equal rights for African Americans. They have been successful in many ways. During and after the Civil Rights Movement, opportunities gradually opened up for black Americans. Large cities elected black mayors, the first African American was named to the United States Supreme Court, the first black governor in the nation's history was elected in the South, and voters chose the first black woman to be a U.S. Senator. Twenty years had passed since Dr. Martin Luther King, Jr.'s "I Have a Dream" speech when, in 1983, the first African-American man traveled into space and the first African-American woman was chosen as Miss America.

During these years, black artists, writers, and musicians began to reach audiences of all races and colors. More positive images of African Americans started to appear on movie and television screens. The black men and women who rose to such positions as judges, astronauts, and members of the President's cabinet gave young African Americans role models to follow.

However, in spite of successes in many areas, there are still black men and women who must struggle to get ahead. In their efforts to overcome obstacles, they are inspired by the people you are reading about in this book. In years to come, they will have an even longer list of African-American achievers to bring them hope and pride.

Andrew Young

Andrew Young was born in 1932 in New Orleans, Louisiana, where his father was a successful dentist. Andrew was such an excellent student that he graduated from high school when he was only fifteen years old. He went on to earn a degree from Howard University four years later. He then became a Congregational minister, and traveled to the southern states of Georgia and Alabama, where he preached in rural churches. He was so shocked by the terrible poverty of African Americans who lived in those states that he became active in the Civil Rights Movement, working for better housing and schools for black people in the South, and helping them gain the right to vote.

In 1961, Andrew Young joined a civil rights organization called the Southern Christian Leadership Conference, where he worked closely with Dr. Martin Luther King, Jr., in his efforts to improve conditions for black Americans. In 1972, Young entered politics, becoming the first African American elected to the House of Representatives from Georgia in 101 years.

In 1977, President Jimmy Carter appointed Andrew Young the first African-American ambassador to the United Nations. He later served as mayor of Atlanta, Georgia, for eight years, starting in 1982, and was a leader in bringing the 1996 Summer Olympics to his city.

L. Douglas Wilder

L. Douglas Wilder

On January 13, 1990, Lawrence Douglas Wilder was sworn in as governor of Virginia. He was the first African American to be elected governor in the United States. Wilder was born in Richmond, Virginia, in 1930, the grandson of slaves. His parents named him after Frederick Douglass, an African American who had fought to end slavery, and Paul Laurence Dunbar, a famous black poet. By the time he was twenty, Wilder had graduated from Virginia Union University. He was then drafted into the army and sent to Korea, where he won a Bronze Star for heroism.

After he returned home, Douglas Wilder decided to study law, but he had to leave the state to do so because at that time Virginia did not allow African Americans to attend its law schools. He graduated from Howard University School of Law in Washington, D.C., and returned to Virginia to open an office. He worked for poor people without charging them any money, but he also represented very wealthy people.

Wilder entered politics in 1969 and was elected the first African-American state senator in Virginia since just after the Civil War. During his five terms in the state senate, Wilder worked to end racial discrimination in housing and jobs, and created a state holiday to honor Dr. Martin Luther King, Jr. Wilder made history again in 1985 when he was elected Virginia's first African-American lieutenant governor. Four years later he was elected governor.

Louis Freeman

Louis Freeman is proud of achieving a list of "firsts" that began in 1967 when he was fifteen. That year he and his older brother became two of the first African-American students to attend their high school in Dallas, Texas. They were the first black students in the school's marching band, and Louis was the first African-American corps commander in the ROTC—a military training program for students. In this activity he was inspired by his father, who had been a master sergeant in the U.S. Army. While Louis was in college, at East Texas State University, he earned a license to fly private airplanes. He enjoyed flying his friends around the Texas skies, but at that time he never imagined that someday he would fly airplanes as a career.

After earning a college degree in sociology and psychology, Freeman decided to join the air force. He didn't pass the test he needed to be accepted, and that upset him because he wasn't used to failing. He studied hard and learned everything he could about airplanes. He took the test again and passed. Once in the air force, he received his pilot training at Reese Air Force Base in Texas. The more he learned, the more he enjoyed being a pilot.

Freeman flew planes for the air force for five years. In 1980, he left the military service to become the first African-American pilot to fly for Southwest Airlines, which has headquarters in Dallas, Texas. After twelve years with the airline, Louis Freeman was chosen to be the chief

CAPT. LOUIS FREEMAN

pilot of Southwest's new base in Chicago. He became the first African-American chief pilot for a major airline. In this important job, he was responsible for overseeing all flight operations of the base.

Pamela Carter

Pamela Carter

In November, 1992, Pamela Fanning Carter was elected the attorney general of the state of Indiana, which means she was put in charge of all legal matters for the state. Pamela Carter was the first African-American woman in the United States to be elected to that position. (Thirty years earlier, Edward Brooke of Massachusetts had become the first African-American man to be elected a state attorney general.)

Pamela grew up in Indianapolis, the daughter of a schoolteacher and a businessman. Her parents always encouraged her to do her best. Her grandfather, who lived to be a hundred-and-one-years old, liked to read law books and shared his readings with Pamela when she was a young girl. She enjoyed these lessons, which were the beginning of her interest in law. Pamela also gives credit to a nun at the school she attended, who taught her to always strive to succeed.

In 1965, when she was fifteen years old, Pamela met Dr. Martin Luther King, Jr., while on a school trip to Chicago. This was a very important event in her life. Dr. King told her to have courage in whatever she did. "I was fascinated that he took the time to talk to me," she said. As she grew older, she never forgot his advice. Pamela was an honor student in high school and college. After graduating from the University of Michigan, she was a social worker for several years. In 1984, she went to school to become a lawyer. She had several important jobs before she was elected the state's attorney general, and worked hard to improve health care for mothers and children.

Mae Jemison

Mae Jemison

In September, 1992, a spacecraft named *Endeavor* was shot into the sky from its launching pad in Cape Canaveral, Florida. One of the seven astronauts riding in this craft was a thirty-five-year-old woman named Dr. Mae Jemison. When she was a young girl growing up in Chicago, Jemison had watched earlier spaceflights on television and knew that someday she, too, would be a space traveler. Her parents stressed education, allowing her to spend hours in the library, reading about astronomy and other sciences, and encouraging her love for science fiction novels.

Jemison finished high school at sixteen and won a scholarship to study at Stanford University in California. There she earned degrees in chemical engineering and African and Afro-American Studies. She went on to receive a medical degree from Cornell University Medical College in New York. As a doctor, she served for several years in the Peace Corps, bringing medical care to people in the African countries of Sierra Leone and Liberia. In 1985, she opened her own medical office in Los Angeles, took more courses in engineering, and applied to be an astronaut. In 1987, out of nearly 2,000 applicants, she was one of fifteen chosen for NASA's astronaut training program.

During Jemison's seven-day flight aboard *Endeavor*, she conducted experiments involving the effects of weightlessness and ways to reduce motion sickness. She carried with her several small art objects from West African countries to symbolize her belief that space belongs to all nations.

CAROL MOSELEY-BRAUN

Carol Moseley-Braun

Carol Moseley-Braun made headlines as well as history in November, 1992, when she became the first African-American woman elected to the United States Senate. The daughter of a police officer and a medical worker, Moseley-Braun grew up in the Hyde Park neighborhood of Chicago, Illinois. She attended schools in that city, earned a law degree from the University of Chicago, and worked for three years in the U.S. Attorney's office. She won a special award for her work in that position.

Carol Moseley-Braun has long been known for bringing people together and getting things done. She gained that reputation early in her career as a member of the Illinois House of Representatives, to which she was elected in 1978. During her ten years as a state lawmaker, she dedicated herself to raising money to improve education for the children of Chicago. She also introduced bills to make sure that black people would be treated fairly when trying to find houses or apartments. In 1987, Moseley-Braun was elected to an office called the Cook County Recorder of Deeds. She was the first woman and the first African American to hold such a high office in that county.

When Moseley-Braun was elected a U.S. Senator in November, 1992, at the age of forty-five, she became only the fourth African American in history to serve in the Senate. She was appointed to the Senate Judiciary Committee, a group of senators whose duties include deciding which people should be confirmed as federal judges.

RITA DOVE

Rita Dove

In May, 1993, Rita Dove was chosen to be the poet laureate of the United States. She was picked for this honor because she was considered to be the leading poet in the nation. She was the country's first African-American poet laureate and, at the age of forty, the youngest ever named. She would serve as poet laureate for one year.

Rita Dove was born in Akron, Ohio. Her father was a successful research chemist and her mother was a homemaker. Both of her parents taught her to love reading. Their house was full of books, and she has said, "I always felt that books were my companions." Her parents hoped that she would study to be a doctor or a lawyer, but Rita decided to become a writer, and to be the best writer that she could be. She earned degrees from Miami University in Ohio and from the University of Iowa. When she was appointed poet laureate, she was an English professor at the University of Virginia.

Rita Dove has published several books of poetry and fiction. In 1987, she received the Pulitzer Prize in poetry for her third book of poems, *Thomas and Beulah*, which was inspired by the lives of her grandparents. Some of her other poetry books are *The Yellow House on the Corner, Museum*, and *Grace Notes*. In her writing, Dove often uses the experiences of African Americans, including herself and her family. She has said that she wishes young people would not be afraid to study poetry, but would think of poems as something to read, listen to, and love.

Ronald Brown

During the years before he was killed in an airplane crash in 1996, Ronald Brown achieved many "firsts." He was the first African American to join a fraternity at his college, the first to head a major political party, and the first to become a partner in the law firm where he worked. Born in Washington, D.C., in 1941, Brown, whose friends called him Ron, grew up in New York City. His father was the manager of the Hotel Theresa in the neighborhood of Harlem. Brown spent much of his childhood living at the hotel and meeting the politicians, sports figures, and entertainers who often stayed there. He attended private schools in New York, and then enrolled in Middlebury College in Vermont, where he was the first black student to join a fraternity.

After graduation, Brown enlisted in the army, reaching the rank of captain. He left to attend law school, then moved to Washington, D.C., to work for a civil rights organization called the Urban League, where he stayed for twelve years. He became active in politics, and in 1989, he was elected chairman of the Democratic National Committee. In that job, he helped guide President Bill Clinton to victory in 1992. In turn, Clinton chose Ron Brown as the first African-American Secretary of Commerce. In April, 1996, on a mission for the Commerce Department, Brown and thirty-two others were killed when their plane crashed while trying to land at an airport in the republic of Croatia.

First African American to win the Nobel Prize in Literature

Toni Morrison

"I'm thrilled that my mother is still alive and can share this with me," said author Toni Morrison in October, 1993, when she won the Nobel Prize in Literature for her novels about African-American life. Both Morrison's mother and father had introduced her to books when she was very young, teaching her to read before she started first grade. By the time she entered high school, she knew she wanted to go on to college. She left the city of Lorain, Ohio, where she had been born in 1931, and enrolled at Howard University in Washington, D.C. She earned a degree in English from Howard and then a master's degree from Cornell University in New York State.

In 1965, Toni Morrison became an editor for a New York publishing company, and five years later she published her first novel, *The Bluest Eye*, about a young African-American girl who wished she could have blue eyes. Morrison published three more books in the next eleven years—*Sula, Song of Solomon*, and *Tar Baby*. Her 1987 novel, *Beloved*, the story of a runaway slave, was a great success and earned Morrison a Pulitzer Prize.

By the time she won the Nobel Prize, she had published six novels and a book of essays. Morrison said she chose to write about the experiences of African-American girls and women because there had been so few books that told about their lives.

Beverly Harvard

Beverly Harvard still remembers the first African-American police officer in her hometown of Macon, Georgia. He was the brother of her best friend, and she recalls the family's big celebration when he was hired by the police department. Beverly had no thoughts of becoming a police officer herself until she had grown up, graduated from college, gotten married, and was living in Atlanta, the capital city of Georgia.

In the early 1970s, Beverly Harvard and her husband were at a party when the conversation turned to the idea of hiring women as police officers. One person remarked that the police department should only hire women who were very tall and weighed more than 200 pounds. Beverly was surprised to hear her husband agree. On the way home from the party, she bet him $100 that she, a short and slender woman, could become a police officer. She soon won the bet by joining the Atlanta police department. She moved up steadily through the department, holding numerous jobs. In 1994, twenty years after she started out as a patrol officer, the mayor of Atlanta chose Beverly Harvard to be chief of police, the first African-American woman police chief in any big city in the country.

As head of the police department, Harvard has started new programs to protect the residents of Atlanta, and she played an important role during the 1996 Olympic Games. She advises children that they can reach their goals by being prepared, working hard, and never turning down a chance to get ahead. She admits that when she was

BEVERLY HARVARD

growing up she was lucky to have parents, sisters, and brothers who always gave her love and support.

INDEX

Page numbers in italics indicate illustrations

GAYLORD S